THE STORY BEHIND

WOOL

Christin Ditchfield

Heinemann Library
Chicago, Illinois

www.heinemannraintree.com

Visit our website to find out more information about Heinemann-Raintree books.

To order:

☎ Phone 888-454-2279

💻 Visit www.heinemannraintree.com to browse our catalog and order online.

Edited by Megan Cotugno and Diyan Leake
Designed by Philippa Jenkins
Original illustrations © Capstone Global
   Library Ltd (2012)
Illustrated by Philippa Jenkins
Picture research by Hannah Taylor and Mica Brancic
Originated by Capstone Global Library Ltd
Printed and bound in China by CTPS

15 14 13 12 11
10 9 8 7 6 5 4 3 2 1

Library of Congress Cataloging-in-Publication Data
Ditchfield, Christin.
   The story behind wool / Christin Ditchfield.
      p. cm.—(True stories)
   Includes bibliographical references and index.
   ISBN 978-1-4329-5436-9 (hardcover)
   1. Wool—Juvenile literature. 2. Wool—History—Juvenile literature. 3. Wool industry—Juvenile literature. I. Title.
   TS1547.D58 2012
   677'.31—dc22   2010044354

Acknowledgments
We would like to thank the following for permission to reproduce photographs: Alamy pp. 7 (© Ted Foxx), 10 (© Bildarchiv Monheim GmbH), 11 (© North Wind Picture Archives), 12 (© Mary Evans Picture Library), 14 (© Wildlight Photo Agency), 17 (© Guy Croft Industrial), 25 (© Travel Scotland - Paul White); Corbis pp. 18 (Reuters/Tara Todras-Whitehill), 21 (Nigel Cattlin/Visuals Unlimited); iStockphoto pp. 20 (© John Krajewski), 27 (© omgimages); Photolibrary pp. 6 (Imagesource), 8 (Vivienne Sharp), 13 (Photononstop/ Herve Gyssels); Shutterstock pp. iii (© Luis Francisco Cordero), 4 (© Richard Peterson), 5 (© BasPhoto), 15 (© Clearviewstock), 16 (© Chris Turner), 19 (© Olga A), 23 (© 1000 Words), 24 (© THP | Tim Hester Photography), 26 (© Moreno Soppelsa).

Cover photograph of a close-up view of a yellow knitted hat reproduced with permission of Corbis (ZenShui/© Michele Constantini).

We would like to thank Ann Fullick for her invaluable help in the preparation of this book.

Every effort has been made to contact copyright holders of material reproduced in this book. Any omissions will be rectified in subsequent printings if notice is given to the publisher.

Disclaimer

Contents

Some words are shown in bold, **like this**.
You can find out what they mean by
looking in the glossary on page 30.

What Is Wool?

▲ This is "raw" wool, straight from the sheep. It has not yet been processed or treated in any way.

When you cuddle up under a cozy blanket, pull your favorite sweater over your head, or grab your hat and mittens to go and play outside, you may be feeling the warmth of wool. Wool is the soft, thick, curly hair of sheep and other animals.

Did you know?

Sheep helped make the spread of **civilization** possible! Once people learned how to use sheep's wool to make warm clothing, they could travel to cooler climates and live in places with colder temperatures. They also knew that if they took their flocks of sheep with them, they would have a reliable source of food.

A sheep's hair or fur is also called its **fleece**. Different kinds of sheep have different kinds of fleece. Some is softer than others. Some is thicker and some is longer. Sheep farmers **breed** their sheep (raise a particular kind of sheep) to produce the kind of fleece they want. Once a year, in the spring, the farmers **shear** their sheep. They use special clippers to cut off the heavy fleece. It's like giving the sheep a haircut!

Later, the wool **fibers** of the sheep's fleece will be turned into wool and fabric, and used to make all kinds of things.

Where wool comes from

Most wool comes from sheep. Cashmere is a kind of wool that comes from goat hair. Mohair comes from goats, camels, and South American animals called llamas, alpaca, and vicuna. Angora is made of rabbit fur.

▼ **This farmer is shearing his sheep with electric clippers.**

 Wool can be made into warm hats, mittens, and blankets.

What makes wool special?

Wool **fiber** has many special qualities or **characteristics**. It is much stronger than many other natural fibers, so it doesn't easily break. Wool cloth or fabric can be stretched, pulled, or draped (hung loosely). Once it has been washed, it returns to its original shape.

Wool fabric **resists** wrinkling. It traps heat, keeping people who are wearing wool warm. Wool fiber soaks up moisture from the air. This makes it fire-resistant. Wool also easily absorbs (soaks up) dye. It can be made any color you like.

What wool is used for

Wool can be made into all kinds of clothing—socks, sweaters, skirts, pants, and suits. It is also used to make warm winter underwear, gloves, hats, and scarves.

People sleep on wool mattresses, under wool blankets, or in wool sleeping bags. They sit on wool car seat covers and walk on wool rugs and carpets. Sometimes wool is even used to cushion the inner working parts of heavy machinery or quiet the sounds coming from stereo speakers or pianos.

Safety first

Wool doesn't easily catch fire. When it does, it doesn't melt, drip, or give off poisonous smoke. As the fabric burns, it creates a kind of ash that puts the fire out. That's why wool is often used to make uniforms for fire fighters, soldiers, and others who work in dangerous environments.

◀ On the inside of this piano, wool coverings soften the sound of the keys and reduce any buzzing noise.

The History of Wool

▲ Early civilizations learned to breed sheep for their wool, as well as their meat.

As early as 10,000 BCE, sheep farmers in central Asia were raising and **breeding** sheep for meat and milk. It wasn't until sometime between 5000 and 3000 BCE that early **civilizations** learned to take the sheep's wool and **spin** (twist) it into **yarn** or thread. Then they could use it to make cloth. From cloth they could make coverings such as tents, blankets, and clothing.

At first, people used very simple tools to spin the yarn. These included wooden spikes or sticks called spindles.

In time, nearly every civilization developed some method of spinning wool. These included the Hebrews of Mesopotamia (the area now called Iraq), the ancient Egyptians, the ancient Greeks, the Babylonians and Persians, and the Romans. Sheep breeding and wool production techniques then spread through Great Britain and northern Europe.

The Roman era

By 200 BCE, the Romans were breeding sheep specifically for wool production. They mated the sheep that had the best wool, so that their offspring would have even better wool. The earliest wool factory was established in the town of Winchester, England, in 50 CE, under Roman rule.

People used **looms** to weave wool thread into cloth. A loom is a frame made of wood. Wool **fibers** are stretched on the frame. This is called the warp. Then more wool fibers are stretched in and out of the warp in a series of rows called the weft. The criss-cross pattern is called weaving. This is how cloth is made.

▼ **This diagram shows how the weft is woven through the warp.**

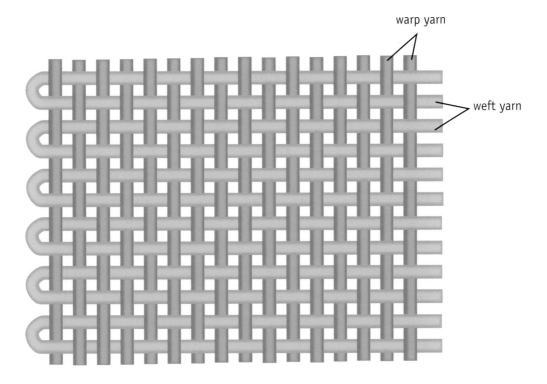

warp yarn

weft yarn

9

▲ This photograph shows the kind of loom that was used to weave cloth in the Middle Ages.

The Middle Ages

In the Middle Ages (500–1500 CE), wool production became a major **industry** (business). Countries such as Spain, France, Italy, and Belgium began to develop new sheep **breeding** and weaving techniques. Great Britain rose above them all. Its "empire of wool" made its rulers rich and powerful. Today, the Lord Speaker of the House of Lords of the British parliament still speaks from the Woolsack. This is a large, wool-stuffed seat that represents the importance of the wool trade as a symbol of Great Britain's wealth.

Over time, quarrels over the wool trade led to political conflicts. Rulers passed laws forcing people to wear expensive wool clothing on special occasions. Wool traders had to pay high fees to buy or sell wool from country to country. Laws stated that sheep farms could be seized by the government for minor offenses.

Colonial times

The explorer Christopher Columbus brought sheep to North America on his second voyage in 1493. The **colonists** began raising sheep in Jamestown, Virginia, in the early 1600s.

The British saw wool production in the colonies as a threat to their business, so they made laws against it. (The punishment was to have a hand cut off!) This and other unfair laws led to the American Revolution in 1776, and the creation of the United States as an independent nation.

A funny expression

To have "the wool pulled over your eyes" means to be fooled or deceived. Some people say it comes from a time when judges in the United States wore wool wigs. A judge fooled by a clever lawyer was said to have "the wool" (his wig) pulled over his eyes so that he couldn't see the details of the case clearly.

◄ People in the colonies made their own wool to avoid buying it from Great Britain.

▲ This spinning jenny could do the job of 16 people.

The industrial age

During the Industrial Revolution of 1750–1850, many new inventions dramatically affected every aspect of the wool **industry**. Machines powered by steam and electricity replaced the old machines that were powered by hand. The new machines could produce better quality wool faster than ever before.

James Hargreaves invented the spinning jenny in 1764. A factory worker could use this multi-**spool** spinning wheel to create eight spools of wool thread at a time, instead of only one. In the early 1800s, there were riots in some towns. Workers feared that these new machines would replace them and cost them their jobs, but there was no going back to the old ways. The new technology was just too good.

The modern era

In the last 100 years, **manufacturers** (people who make products to sell) have experimented with new kinds of wool and new methods of making it. Even greater improvements have been made in the technology used by wool mills and factories. Today, nearly all spinning and weaving is done by machines programmed by computers. They can produce in minutes the kind of wool thread and wool fabric that used to take people days, weeks, or even months. Yet there are people all over the world who still use traditional methods to weave cloth for themselves and their families.

▼ This modern machine spins wool in a factory in France.

Different Kinds of Wool

▲ Wool classers sort the wool into bins.

Today when a sheep has been **sheared**, a worker called a wool classer examines the **fleece** to determine the quality of the wool. He or she separates the wool into classes or grades, according to thickness, quantity, quality, and strength. Grades of wool include coarse (rough), strong, medium, fine, superfine, and ultrafine. (The word *fine* is used to mean "thin" or "delicate.") The finest wool is the thinnest, smoothest, and softest wool.

Once the wool has been turned into fabric, it falls into one of two categories: **woolens** or **worsteds**. Woolens are spun from shorter, thicker wool **fibers**. They look fluffy or fuzzy and feel thick and bulky. Woolens make heavy coats, jackets, and sweaters, as well as blankets and carpets.

Worsteds are spun from longer, thinner wool fibers. The fabric feels smooth and lightweight. Worsteds are made into suits, pants, skirts, and dresses. Worsted **yarn** can be used to create beautiful **embroidery**. It is also the most expensive!

The money's in Merino

Merino wool is the softest, finest wool of all. It comes from Merino sheep, which were originally bred in Spain. Most sheep sell for under $200, but in 2008, a buyer paid $14,000 for one Australian Merino sheep with especially fine wool.

▼ Fine merino wool fibers are about 1½ to 3 inches (4 to 7.5 centimeters) long.

Working with Wool

▲ **Freshly sheared wool contains sand, dirt, grease, and dried sweat.**

Wool that comes straight from sheep is called "raw" wool or "grease" wool. Once the sheep have been sheared and the wool has been graded, it needs to be washed and scoured.

The wool is given several baths in water, soap, and soda ash (a cleaning material made from salt). A waxy substance called **lanolin** is removed from the **fleece** and set aside. Later it will be sold to cosmetic companies for use in creams and lotions.

Giant rollers squeeze excess water out of the wool. Sometimes oil is added as a kind of conditioner, to make the wool softer, smoother, and easier to work with. Next, the wool is placed into a **carding** (combing) machine. The machine has a series of metal teeth that work like combs to smooth the wool **fibers** and blend them together.

Carded wool goes to the spinning machine. Individual strands of wool fiber are spun together. The machine twists and retwists them until they form strings of **yarn**. The yarn is wound around spindles or cylinders that are sometimes called bobbins.

Dying wool

Dyes can be added to give wool color at almost any stage in the process: before or after carding, spinning, or weaving. It's up to the **manufacturer** to decide what will work best for the type of wool product they are making.

▼ **This giant carding machine is combing wool fibers to smooth them and blend them together.**

From yarn to fabric

The wool yarn then is made into fabric. One kind of machine weaves yarn spun from the longer, thinner fibers into **worsteds**. Another kind of machine knits yarn spun from the shorter, thicker fibers into **woolens**.

▲ This is a circular knitting machine used in a clothing factory in Cairo, Egypt.

Wool blends

Sometimes wool fibers are blended with other fibers, such as cotton, silk, or **rayon**. These blended fabrics have the best qualities of each of the original fibers. By law, clothing manufacturers are required to include labels that show whether an item is made of "pure wool" or a blend. These labels also include instructions on how best to care for the fabrics.

Then the fabric is put through a process called fulling, or milling. This process tightens the weave and improves the texture of the fabric. It also preshrinks the fabric, so that it won't shrink after it has been sewn into clothing and blankets.

Another way to preshrink the fabric is to treat it with special **chemicals**. Chemicals can also be used to make the wool more fire-resistant, more water-resistant, and more stain-resistant. Now the fabric is finished and ready to be put to use!

▼ Labels like these use symbols to show how wool fabric should be cared for.

Wearing Wool

▲ Wool sweaters can keep you warm when you play outdoors. The fabric is "breathable," which means that air flows through it, and it doesn't get sweaty and damp.

Wool clothing is often more expensive than clothing made of other fabrics, but it lasts longer and looks less worn over time. Of course, to get the most out of wool clothing, it is important to take good care of it.

Wool doesn't hang on to sweat, dirt, and stains as much as other fabrics do. It doesn't have to be washed after every use. Using a soft brush or a damp cloth, and with a little bit of detergent, you can usually loosen and remove any little spots or stains.

When wool clothing is hung in a closet or folded neatly in a drawer, any wrinkles will usually fall out on their own—no ironing required! Hanging the garment in a steamy bathroom is another way to get rid of wrinkles quickly.

When a wool garment does need a thorough cleaning, most **manufacturers** recommend dry cleaning (the use of **chemicals** to clean instead of soap and water). Putting wool in the washing machine will usually damage the fabric. The **fibers** get fuzzy and lose their shape. In the heat of a clothes dryer, they shrink.

Some wool clothing can be washed by hand and laid flat to dry. Superwash wool is wool that has been treated with chemicals so that it can be machine washed and dried.

Watch out!

Wool that won't be worn for some time should be cleaned and stored in airtight containers, so that moths can't get to it. These insects like to lay their eggs in wool. When the young insects hatch, they eat the wool fibers!

▼ **This moth larva can cause a lot of damage!**

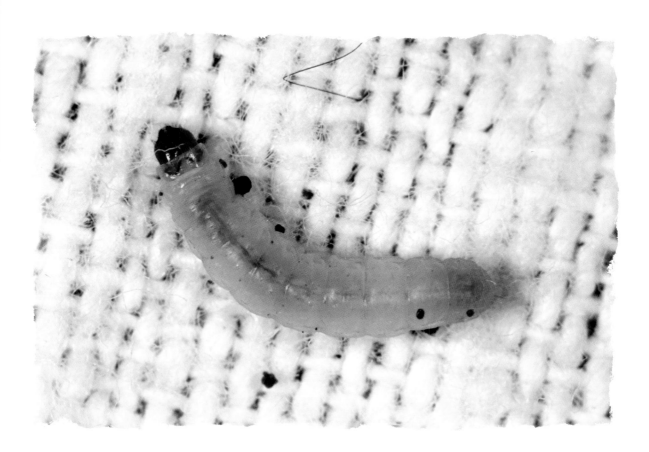

The Business of Wool

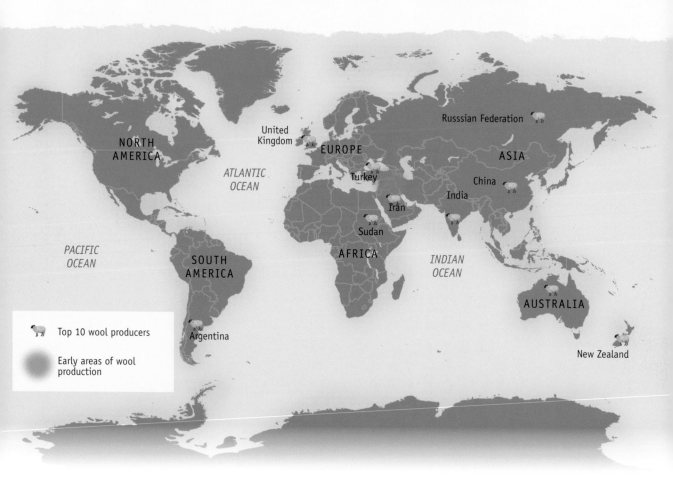

Top 10 wool producers

Early areas of wool production

NORTH AMERICA

ATLANTIC OCEAN

PACIFIC OCEAN

SOUTH AMERICA

Argentina

United Kingdom

EUROPE

Turkey

Iran

Sudan

AFRICA

Russsian Federation

ASIA

China

India

INDIAN OCEAN

AUSTRALIA

New Zealand

▲ All together, the countries of the world produce more than 5.5 billion pounds (2,487,000 metric tons) of wool each year. More than 60 percent of that wool is used to make clothing.

All over the world, wool is big business. The **industry** employs hundreds of thousands of people. Australia produces the most wool—as much as one-quarter of the world's supply. Next come China and New Zealand.

Environmentally friendly

Sheep are good for the environment! They eat all kinds of grass, plants, and weeds that other animals won't touch. When sheep clear out a field or a forest, there's no need to use **pesticides** or mowing equipment. Sheep keep **vegetation** from growing out of control, so it doesn't choke out other plants and trees, or cause a fire hazard.

Sheep in the U.S. and elsewhere

There are 5 million sheep living on 82,000 sheep farms in the United States. Of all 50 states, Texas, California, Colorado, and Wyoming produce the most wool. There are many different breeds of sheep, with certain breeds suited to different areas. For example, there are sheep that are better able to withstand the cold. Wool is popular in the United Kingdom. There are 40 million sheep living on 75,000 sheep farms in the UK.

Let's go shopping!

The United States produces very little wool compared to other countries. However, Americans buy and use more wool than the people of any other country. The United Kingdom comes second on the list, and Japan is third.

▼ The green **pastures** of parts of the United Kingdom are ideal for raising sheep.

It's all about the sheep

A sheep can grow anywhere from 2 to 30 pounds (1 to 14 kilograms) of **fleece** each year. The amount of wool depends on the type of sheep. It also depends on how old the sheep is, how big it is, and how healthy it is—as well as how often it gets **sheared**.

A valuable resource

Sheep give us more than wool. They produce milk used for making cheese, yogurt, and ice cream. The **lanolin** in their fleece is used to manufacture makeup. Sheep are also a good source of meat. Sheepskins can be used to make a special kind of paper, as well as clothing and furniture. Other parts of the sheep are used in medical supplies, musical instruments, and sports equipment.

There are more than 200 types or breeds of sheep. Most of them belong in one of three groups: long wool sheep, medium wool sheep, and fine wool sheep. Sheep farmers choose to raise the breed of sheep that will give them the kind of wool they want to produce and sell.

For centuries, sheep dogs have been used to move sheep from **pasture** to pasture. At festivals called sheep dog trials, these highly trained animals get a chance to show off their special skills. At other fairs and festivals, sheep farmers display their most prized sheep and compete for honors and awards given to those who produce the finest wool. There are sheep-shearing contests to see who can shear the most sheep in the least amount of time.

▼ **This man and his dog are competing at the sheep dog trials in Gairloch, in northwest Scotland.**

The Future of Wool

▲ For thousands of years, wool has been one of the world's most important natural resources.

Millions of people make their living and support their families through their work in the wool **industry**. In the last 50 years, however, wool has had to compete against new **synthetic** (human-made) **fibers** and fabrics. Clothing, blankets, rugs, and other things that used to be made of wool are now being made of acrylic, acetate, nylon, spandex, **rayon**, and polyester. These are all artificial or synthetic fabrics, which are much cheaper to make and cheaper to buy than wool.

The **United Nations** called 2009 the International Year of Natural Fibers to remind people worldwide about the benefits of natural fibers such as wool. In addition to its other special qualities, wool is a very environmentally friendly fabric. Unlike most synthetic fabrics, wool can be renewed, reused, and **recycled**. It is even used as insulation, helping to keep a comfortable temperature inside houses.

Unlike synthetic fabrics, wool is completely **biodegradable**. This means that at the end of its life, wool breaks down and becomes part of the natural environment. As more people "go green" and make choices that are better for the environment, wool is making a comeback.

The knitting craze

In the last ten years, many people have rediscovered the joy of knitting. It's a fun and relaxing hobby. You can make your own socks, sweaters, hats, or scarves in any color or pattern you like. You can make gifts for your friends and family. Some people knit scarves and hats for the homeless or blankets and sweaters for needy children.

◀ Knitting with wool is a fun and enjoyable hobby for people of all ages.

Timeline

(These dates are often approximations.)

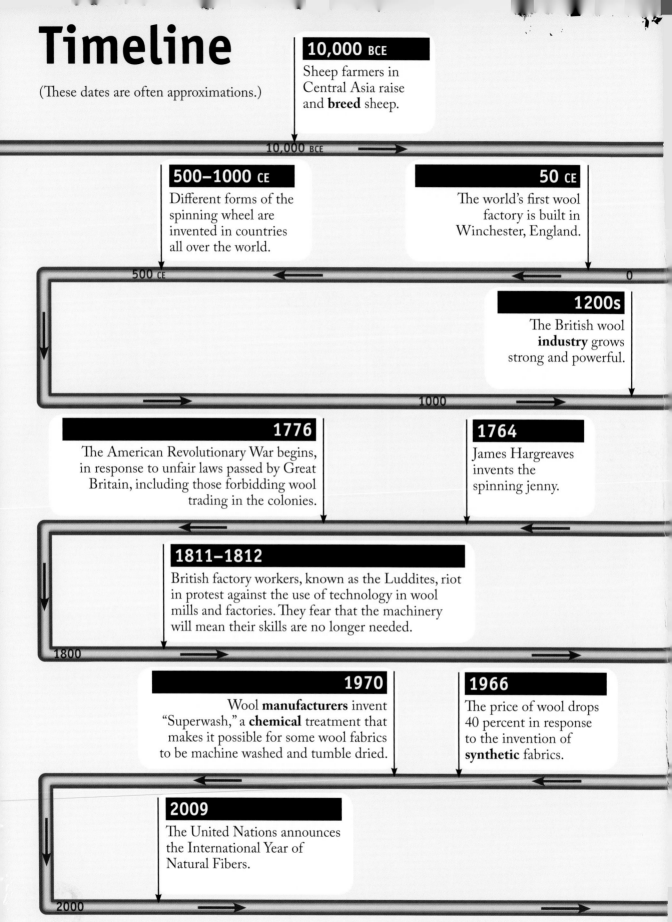

10,000 BCE
Sheep farmers in Central Asia raise and **breed** sheep.

10,000 BCE →

500–1000 CE
Different forms of the spinning wheel are invented in countries all over the world.

50 CE
The world's first wool factory is built in Winchester, England.

500 CE ←   ←   0

1200s
The British wool **industry** grows strong and powerful.

1000 →

1776
The American Revolutionary War begins, in response to unfair laws passed by Great Britain, including those forbidding wool trading in the colonies.

1764
James Hargreaves invents the spinning jenny.

1811–1812
British factory workers, known as the Luddites, riot in protest against the use of technology in wool mills and factories. They fear that the machinery will mean their skills are no longer needed.

1800 →

1970
Wool **manufacturers** invent "Superwash," a **chemical** treatment that makes it possible for some wool fabrics to be machine washed and tumble dried.

1966
The price of wool drops 40 percent in response to the invention of **synthetic** fabrics.

2009
The United Nations announces the International Year of Natural Fibers.

2000 →

⋀⋀⋀ This symbol shows where there is a change of scale in the timeline, or where a long period of time with no noted events has been left out.

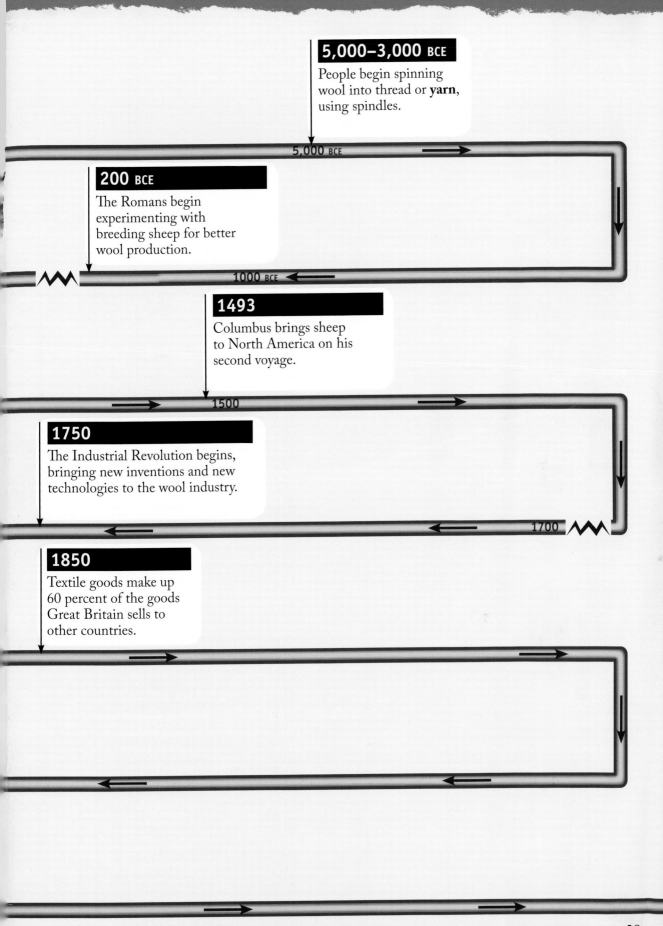

5,000–3,000 BCE

People begin spinning wool into thread or **yarn**, using spindles.

5,000 BCE

200 BCE

The Romans begin experimenting with breeding sheep for better wool production.

1000 BCE

1493

Columbus brings sheep to North America on his second voyage.

1500

1750

The Industrial Revolution begins, bringing new inventions and new technologies to the wool industry.

1700

1850

Textile goods make up 60 percent of the goods Great Britain sells to other countries.

Glossary

biodegradable able to rot away naturally

breed raise a particular type of animal

card comb wool to untangle it so that the wool is ready to be spun

characteristic thing that makes a substance special or different from others

chemical substance that can be made into other substances by changing its atoms or molecules

civilization way of life of a group of people

colonist person who lives in a territory controlled by another nation

embroidery pattern sewn into a fabric for decoration

fiber long, thin thread of a material

fleece sheep's hair or fur; also called wool

industry business or trade

lanolin waxy yellow substance found in sheep wool

loom machine for weaving cloth from thread

manufacturer person or company that makes products to sell

pasture field or land where animals feed on grass

pesticide chemical used to kill harmful insects and other pests

rayon artificial fiber made from wood

recycle use over again—sometimes in a new way

resist fight against, keep out, or prevent something

shear clip or cut with scissors; to remove the fleece of a sheep

spin twist wool into long pieces of yarn or thread

spool cylinder around which thread is wound

synthetic substance that is human-made (from chemicals), not found in nature

United Nations international organization that works to increase cooperation among countries to promote peace and the well-being of people around the world

vegetation grass and plants

woolen fabric knitted from yarn spun from short, thick wool fibers

worsted fabric woven from yarn spun from long, thin wool fibers

yarn fibers that have been twisted or spun into long strands to use in knitting or weaving

Find Out More

Books

Blaxland, Wendy. *Sweaters: How Are They Made?* New York: Benchmark Books, 2010.

Gleason, Carrie. *The Biography of Wool: How Did That Get Here?* New York: Crabtree Publishing Company, 2007.

Oxlade, Chris. *How We Use Wool.* Chicago: Heinemann-Raintree, 2005.

Storey, Rita. *How We Use Materials: Wool and Cotton.* Mankato, MN: Smart Apple Media, 2007.

Websites

www.historyforkids.org/learn/clothing/wool.htm
This site has a lot of helpful links and photos—and even videos of sheep shearing!

http://www.madehow.com/Volume-1/Wool.html
This website has all kinds of detailed information, drawings, and diagrams to help you understand how wool is made.

www.berkshirehistory.com/kids/cloth_making.html
This web page reveals how cloth was made in medieval times.

Places to visit

You can find local factories to visit by searching online for "woolen mills" in your area. There are woolen mills in several states that offer tours of their operations. There are also national wool museums all over Australia and in Scotland and Wales in the United Kingdom. Many of their websites include photos, videos, and virtual tours of their exhibits. So, if you can't travel to one of these museums in those countries, visit them online!

Index